T0356656

THE ALPHABET ABOUT NOTHING

Words by Robin Feiner

Aa

A is for **A**aron the close-talker. With no sense of personal space, Aaron stands just inches away from people's faces when speaking to them. While he briefly dated Elaine, it was Jerry's parents he fell in love with, becoming very emotional at the airport when they flew home.

B is for **B**abu Bhatt.
The proud owner of the
Dream Café, Babu takes Jerry's
advice to serve food from
his home country of Pakistan
and goes out of business.
Jerry tries to help but makes
things worse, leading Babu to
proclaim: 'You very bad man!'

C is for Estelle **C**ostanza. With only one volume — loud and shrill — George's mother is often heard yelling, even when she's speaking on the phone. While she loves her son, she has a funny way of showing it, making fun of him and even calling him a 'bum!'

D is for **D**avid Puddy.
Yeah, that's right. Elaine's
on-again, off-again boyfriend,
Puddy is a tall, handsome
mechanic — but don't call him
a grease monkey. David squints,
stares, likes to give high-fives
and really loves the New Jersey
Devils — proudly painting his
face to support the team.

E is for **E**laine Benes. Get out! Elaine is smart, strong and sassy, but may be the worst dancer in all of New York City. The self-appointed Queen of the Castle, Elaine loves nothing more than the top of the muffin, the Baltimore Orioles and yada yada yada...

F is for **F**rank Costanza. Serenity Now! With a short temper and a foot odor problem, George's father is a force of nature. He created the Mansierre and a Festivus for the rest of us, complete with an aluminum pole, the Airing of Grievances and the Feats of Strength.

Gg

G is for George Costanza. Cantstandya! Short, stocky and bald, this make-believe architect and marine biologist prides himself on being an expert liar, cheat and cheapskate. He ultimately loses every job, girlfriend and ounce of self-respect he's ever had, but will fight to the death for 'Independent George!'

H is for Helen Seinfeld. Jerry's mother is a proud resident of Del Boca Vista in Florida, where she and husband Morty never miss the early-bird special. In her eyes, Jerry is a great person and the perfect son: 'How could anyone not like him?'

I is for **I**zzy Mandelbaum. It's go time! Despite being 80 years old, Izzy still has a reputation for being as strong as an ox, but his competitive nature lands him in hospital. Izzy owns a Magic Pan restaurant, where each crepe has to be hand-rolled by a Mandelbaum.

J is for **J**erry Seinfeld. Playing himself in this off-beat sitcom that made TV history, Jerry unsympathetically watches his friends run into problems, while he somehow manages to always come out even. Sarcastic and Superman-obsessed, he's the most legendary observational comedian of all time. 'Did you ever notice...'

Kk

K is for Cosmo Kramer.
Busting through the door
unannounced, often in a cloud
of cigar smoke, Kramer is
Jerry's madcap neighbor.
Known for his zany fashion
sense and even zanier antics,
Kramer is a hipster doofus
who chases bizarre ideas and
crazy lawsuits. Giddy-up!

L is for **L**awyer Jackie Chiles.
'Who told you to put the balm on?'
This brash, fast-talking lawyer
is a parody of another legendary
lawyer, Johnnie Cochran. Jackie's
last case is during the hilarious
trial that was the 'Seinfeld' finale,
where he defends Jerry and co.
for being 'innocent bystanders.'

M is for Morty Seinfeld. Jerry's father is a crotchety, impatient man who hates the sound of Velcro. He prides himself on his genius invention: a belt-less trench coat that he named 'The Executive.' Morty thinks it's a classic — but nobody ever bought it.

N is for **N**ewman.
Hello, Newman. He's the chubby, scheming mailman who never works in the rain. With his emphatic, angry rants and the agility of a ring-tailed lemur, perhaps Jerry's sworn enemy is not pure evil, but rather 'an enigma, a mystery wrapped in a riddle.'

O is for the **O**valtine bit by Kenny Bania. An awful comedian who looks up to Jerry, Kenny is known for his infamous bit about Ovaltine. At 12 minutes long, the routine is so bad that Jerry says it's like 'getting beaten with a bag of oranges!'

Pp

P is for Jacopo Peterman. Eccentric, well-traveled and known for his lyrical rhetoric, Elaine's boss and owner of the J. Peterman Catalog brings a certain sophisticated charm to every conversation. His lavish tastes include nothing less than JFK's golf clubs and King Henry VIII's wedding cake!

Q is for Queens.
This is home to the Costanzas, including George himself when times get tough. Attempting to increase his 'buffer zone,' George convinces his parents to move to Florida. 'It's my turn to live, baby!' But his freedom is short-lived when, unfortunately for him, they soon return home to Queens.

Rr

R is for Ray and Bob.
Ray — who also goes by
Cedric — and Bob are two
street toughs that seem to
torment Kramer! Whether
they're stealing an armoire
from him, making him wear
a ribbon or chasing him
through the streets, Kramer
always ends up on the
wrong side of this pair.

S is for the **S**oup Nazi. Chef Yev Kassem makes delicious soup, but you need to follow his strict rules if you want a taste. While he only appears in two episodes, the Soup Nazi served up perhaps the most famous catchphrase in the show's history: 'No soup for you!'

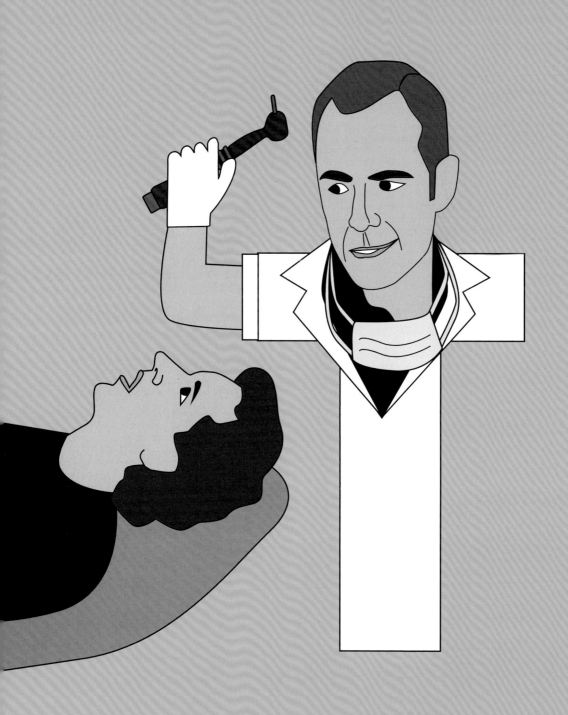

T is for **T**im Whatley. Dentist to the stars, Tim is a re-gifter who is interested in Elaine and keeps questionable reading material in his waiting room. Jerry suspects that Tim later converted to Judaism just for the jokes, which offended Jerry not as a Jew, but as a comedian!

U is for **U**ncle Leo.
'Jerry! Hello!' Don't let
Uncle Leo's warm welcome
fool you — once he grabs hold
of your arm, you could be
stuck talking to him for hours.
The brother of Helen Seinfeld,
Leo is a notorious cheapskate
who steals from his family and
finds watches in trashcans.

V is for Dr. Van Nostrand. Dr. Martin van Nostrand from the clinic is a physician with highly questionable skills and credentials. While the doctor claims to be a Juilliard trained dermatologist, he's actually just Kramer smoking a pipe or wearing a white coat.

W is for Sally **W**eaver.
She's Susan Ross' old college
roommate who moves to New
York to become an actress.
But when Kramer tells her
that Jerry thinks she should
just give up, she turns on
Jerry and finds success with
a one-woman show called
'Jerry Seinfeld is the Devil.'

X is for Xmas vs. Festivus. Some people just don't like Christmas. That's why Frank Costanza invented Festivus... 'Festivus for the rest of us.' What could be more fun than a round of 'Airing of the Grievances?'

Yy

Y is for **Y**ankees' owner George Steinbrenner. Based on the real-life owner of New York's famous baseball team, Steinbrenner never stops talking. While we only ever see the back of his head, the motor-mouth millionaire has an instantly recognizable voice, provided by 'Seinfeld' co-creator, Larry David.

Zz

Z is for Dr. **Z**hang Zhao's Baldness Cure. George sees a commercial on late-night television for a miraculous baldness medicine from Beijing. With translation help from Ping — the Chinese delivery boy — George places an order. When it arrives, boy, does it stink.

The ever-expanding legendary library

EXPLORE THESE LEGENDARY ALPHABETS & MORE AT WWW.ALPHABETLEGENDS.COM

THE ALPHABET ABOUT NOTHING
www.alphabetlegends.com

Published by Alphabet Legends Pty Ltd in 2024
Created by Beck Feiner
Copyright © Alphabet Legends Pty Ltd 2024

Printed and bound in China.

978-0-9756692-7-3